RAFFLES HOTEL *Style*

PUBLISHED BY
Raffles Hotel (1886) Ltd
A Raffles International Hotel

EDITOR
Jill A. Laidlaw

ART DIRECTOR
Tan Tat Ghee

DESIGNER
Tan Seok Lui

ACKNOWLEDGEMENTS
The hotel would like to thank the following for their
gracious assistance in the preparation of this book:
David Lim of Cheong Ann Watch Maker; Julie Yeo of
Antiques of the Orient; A. Raham Talib formerly of
Hassan's Carpets; Anthony Lee of Just Anthony and
Ah Kheng of Tong Mern Sern.

PRODUCED BY
EDITIONS DIDIER MILLET
593, Havelock Road #02-01/02
Isetan Office Building,
Singapore 169641
E-mail: edm@pacific. net. sg
Tel: 65-735 7990
Fax: 65-735 8981

© 1997 Raffles Hotel (1886) Ltd

Printed in Singapore by Tien Wah Press (Pte) Ltd
ISBN 981-3018-86-0

All Rights Reserved. No part of this book may
be reproduced, stored in a retrieval system,
or transmitted in any form or by any means
without permission from the publisher.

Title page: *The RH
monogram roundel. This
stained glass decorative
disc is found on the hotel's
cast-iron pavilions and is
based on an original
architectural drawing
found in the Singapore
National Archives.*

Contents: *With its
Chinese antiques and
artworks, the Cathay
Suite is a reminder of
Raffles Hotel's fusion of
East and West — and is
a particular favourite with
guests. The verandah is
a perfect place to relax.*

RAFFLES HOTEL *Style*

TEXT BY
Gretchen Liu

PHOTOGRAPHY BY
Albert Lim K.S.

Contents

CHAPTER 1

The Elements of Style

There are few hotels in the world that are thriving in their second century. Raffles Hotel is one of them. The occasion of Raffles' 110th anniversary is the perfect time to reflect on the elements of style that have endeared the Grand Old Lady to generations of travellers and made it that rare thing in the world today: a true classic. The hotel has, of course, seen its fortunes ebb and flow over the years so some elements of style remain, often thankfully, unique to a particular period. The best, however, have proven remarkably resilient and hark back to Raffles' early heyday when it first became widely known as 'the Finest Caravanserai East of Suez'.

Perhaps the single most enduring and alluring element of Raffles Hotel style is its architecture: an arrangement of low-rise, verandah-enclosed, colonial-style buildings, painted white with terracotta-tiled pitched roofs, set amidst courtyards and gardens. The contrast between the lush and generous tropical gardens and turn-of-the-century colonial architecture has rarely failed to generate an appreciative response. As one visitor in the early thirties put it: 'Besides being a landmark of European civilisation in the hubbub of Asia, the Raffles is a palace among hotels. Compared with the towering piles of New York and Chicago, it would look aged and squat and rambling, but here in the eye of the Orient it is germane to its natural setting.'

The composition of buildings and gardens was the culmination of two decades of steady expansion. The hotel's beginnings were extremely modest. The doors opened on 1 December 1887 in a cavernous Anglo-Indian bungalow with no architectural pretensions. (All of Singapore's other early hotels were similarly housed.) The property was known as Beach House and was owned by the wealthy Arab trader and landowner Syed Mohammed Alsagoff whose father had acquired it from a Scottish family in 1870. There were two aspects of the property which strongly recommended it as a hotel site however: a large compound of garden and an unimpeded view of the sea, then lapping on to the sandy shore on the other side of Beach Road.

The hotel's first advertisement stated that the proprietors were 'confident that the Raffles Hotel will meet a great want long felt in Singapore' and was signed 'Sarkies Brothers'. The four Armenian siblings — Martin, Tigrin, Aviet and Arshak — were already established in the region. Martin, the eldest, started the business in Penang in the 1870s. He opened two hotels, the Eastern and the Oriental, which he merged as the Eastern and Oriental — or E&O — Hotel. Not long after opening Raffles, the brothers ventured to Rangoon (in modern-day Myanmar) and added the Strand Hotel to their empire. The responsibilities of the hotel empire were divided by territory with Tigrin in Singapore, astutely nurturing Raffles' transformation from hostelry to grand hotel with a world renowned reputation.

A formal portrait of Raffles Hotel, circa 1910 (opposite). The butterfly wings were designed to receive guests arriving by horse-drawn gharry while the front verandah was scattered with tables (above) where visitors could enjoy a view of the sea, then lapping at the shore across Beach Road.

Ambitious and farsighted, Tigrin was also a terrific builder. Like other enlightened hoteliers of his generation, he understood that accommodation in the course of travelling need not be a painful necessity but could become an opportunity to indulge in a kind of fantasy world where travellers felt liberated from ordinary responsibilities. The creation of an appropriate setting was thus the first order of the day. During his quarter century running Raffles, there was either a construction site in the grounds or a building project on the drawing board.

The first decade saw two important additions. First came a pair of two storey buildings, one on each side of the old bungalow. (Completed in 1899 and still standing, they were among Singapore's first purpose-built hotel rooms and are the oldest part of Raffles Hotel today.) Soon after, the brothers purchased a large piece of adjacent land along Beach Road and built an L-shaped extension which formed the famous Palm Court. Thus the beginnings of Raffles as we know it today.

Raffles Hotel opened in 1887 in a rather sombre-looking old bungalow (above) known as Beach House. Tropical suits and solar topi were as much a part of Raffles Hotel's early style as bentwood tables and rattan chairs (opposite), here all captured in a rare informal photograph, circa 1912.

The pleasing proportions, the open plan and the long perspectives along the verandahs endowed these early buildings with great classical dignity. In the fashion of the day, the beds were furnished with mosquito nets. Each bedroom was fronted by its own private verandah and backed by the bathroom and ensuite dressing room. Bathroom fittings were minimal but effective. There were no taps. Water was brought by servants who had direct access to the bathroom from the service verandahs and filled the large 'Shanghai jar'. To bathe, water was scooped up from the jar and poured over the body. Night soil was also discreetly removed by the service verandahs. (Although no longer used for such purposes, these timber verandahs are still very much a part of the character of the buildings.)

Yet all of this attention to the comfort of his guests was but a prelude to Tigrin's most ambitious plan: a magnificent structure to replace the old bungalow. The services of Swan & Maclaren, Singapore's preeminent firm of architects, were enlisted in 1897. The signature on the original building plans reveals the hand of R.A.J. Bidwell, the talented London-trained architect who did much to improve the city's skyline around the turn of the century. Two years later, the Main Building made its dazzling debut amidst a shocking blaze of lights.

The completion of the Main Building marked a turning point in Raffles' fortunes. With its good Renaissance manners (Ionic, Doric and Corinthian orders), Palladian windows, endless verandahs and distinctive butterfly wings, the Main Building was immediately considered one of Singapore's finest buildings. Surrounded as it is today by skyscrapers, it is all too easy to forget that it was, by the standards of its day, imposing and frightfully modern. The late Victorian Italianate Revival design was extremely fashionable, the iron-frame construction advanced, and the installation of electricity was

8

considered a marvel. The hotel's own generator powered 800 light bulbs, five arc lamps over the entrance and electric fans in the principal rooms. Indeed, some guests complained that the Drawing Rooms were too bright!

Tigrin then turned his attention to cuisine and, following the great European Belle Epoch hoteliers who were his contemporaries, he elevated the experience of public dining in Singapore to an entirely new level. The inspired setting for his feasts was the new Main Dining Room. It occupied virtually the entire ground floor of the Main Building and was advertised as being 'capable of seating 500'. As the 1913 edition of the popular compendium *Seaports of the Far East* noted: 'The chief glory of the hotel is its magnificent dining hall, overlooked by balconies on the upper floors. Its handsome pillars, its white Carrara marble floor, and the dainty artistic arrangement of its numerous tables form an ensemble unsurpassed outside Europe and America; and at night, when dinner is in progress, to the accompaniment of the excellent orchestra, the gay and festive scene is one to be remembered.'

Greetings from Raffles! Postcards of the Main Dining Room (top), the ballroom set for a cruise dinner (middle) and a classic view of the Palm Court (below). These postcards are part of a popular series produced in the mid-twenties.

And still the building work continued: new kitchens, an enlarged and improved Bar and Billiard Room, a cast-iron verandah and the Bras Basah Wing which boasted shops along the ground floor. By the time of Tigrin Sarkies' death in 1912 Raffles Hotel as we know it today was in place and was hailed as 'the Savoy of Singapore'. His high standards and sense of style have proved to be a lasting, famous and welcome legacy.

It was the interlude between the two World Wars which saw the emergence of the second key element of Raffles Hotel style: the making of myth and legend. As more people travelled the world for pleasure Singapore became the Clapham Junction of the Eastern Seas. Everyone, it seemed, stopped in the port city for at least a day. A visit to Raffles Hotel became one of the rites of passage of world travellers and 'see you at Raffles' an oft-repeated parting shot.

A large ballroom was added in 1920, perfectly capturing the mood of the decade. Most evenings the dance music echoed through the ballroom's high open walls. Outside, along Beach Road, the jinricksha boys rushed and panted as motor cars dashed up to the entrance depositing their 'virile freight of handsome well-dressed men and women'. Dancing was warm work even in the 'coolest ballroom in the East' so intervals were spent at the rattan tables and chairs cosily arranged along the edge of the dance floor drinking Gin *Pahits*, Singapore Slings and Million Dollar Cocktails.

During the day the ballroom was the perfect place to watch the flotsam and jetsam of the port city — deeply tanned rubber planters and tin miners down from

Malaya, officers from ships in port, pale civil servants and middle aged army officers flushed with too much drink. This was the Raffles that fascinated Maugham and Coward. Many have since come in search of Maugham's world and stayed in his favourite suite facing the Palm Court, Suite 102, expecting time to somehow stand still in the sun drenched gardens and cool verandahs.

Yet the hotel was showing signs of age. Although still ranked as one of the best hotels in the East one visitor observed, not without fondness, that it was 'cherished for its Somerset Maugham associations rather than for the distinction of its decor'. The management responded by bestowing a new title on Raffles: 'The historic hotel of Singapore' and so it was labelled on hotel stationery and advertisements. A visitor in 1927 penned his impression thus:

The Hotel Raffles is unique, consisting of a series of capacious buildings around a hollow square and situated amid beautiful foliage and flowers. Its bedrooms, with their generous size and high ceilings, make one think of a courtroom back home. A large, single bladed wooden fan, not unlike the propeller of an airship, is fastened to the ceiling and rotates with such speed that it supplies a much needed breeze in every part of the room. In front of each bedroom is a spacious porch, with table, rockers and armchairs, and a good electric light. This serves as a comfortable sitting room, and shutters screen it from passers-by. Here the boy, a noiseless omnipresent servant, places your morning coffee (which is usually tea) to greet you as you rise, and of which you partake before one of the many daily baths. The bath itself is a stone jar filled with water and is in a large room. With a convenient, short handled dipper, you sluice yourself over with water. When one becomes accustomed to this method of bathing, it is very satisfactory.

The boom years ended abruptly with the Great Depression. Plans to upgrade the hotel were cancelled. One of the casualties of the world slump was the bankruptcy of the Sarkies family firm, headed by the youngest and only surviving Sarkies brother, Arshak, who managed the E&O in Penang but was a frequent visitor to Raffles. As the tangled financial web was unravelled the hotel faced closure by creditors. Disaster was narrowly averted. The public rallied around, the creditors supported the option to keep the hotel open, believing in it's long term viability and, after several months of tough negotiations, a new company, Raffles Hotel Ltd, was formed to run it.

Fame had undoubtedly helped to save the day. Raffles was already acknowledged as an attraction in its own right and as an icon for all that was perceived to be romantic and exotic in travel — 'Immortalized by writers, patronised by all', records the King

Mosquito nets and ceiling fans (above) were essential bedroom furnishings until airconditioning made its appearance in the fifties. But this modern comfort necessitated the lowering of ceilings while the interior decoration became increasingly estranged from its tropical context (below).

11

Restoring Raffles. A multi-national army of craftsmen laboured for two-and-a-half years to return the hotel to its original splendour. The early stages of the restoration revealed an array of colours and patterns (opposite, below). During the final stages the tension quickened as attention turned to details such as the plasterwork on the numerous column capitals (above) and the cast-iron pavilions (opposite, above).

George V Silver Jubilee Souvenir Programme of 1935. Adding lustre to its reputation were the famous guests who visited during the twenties and thirties oblivious to the fluctuations of its fortunes — the Prince of Wales danced in the ballroom as did the new royalty of Hollywood, including Douglas Fairbanks, Mary Pickford, Charlie Chaplin and Pauline Goddard.

Eventually, however, the tropically-friendly architecture proved to be a liability as the management struggled to keep pace with new technology. The installation of modern plumbing in the Main Building required the enclosure of generous verandahs. The advent of airconditioning in the early fifties saw the lowering of ceilings in bedrooms and the walling in of the private verandahs in the older buildings. The interiors were also given modern touches: linoleum floors, wallpapered walls, sleek fifties furniture, chenille bedspreads and chrome light fixtures.

Fast forward to the late eighties. Having survived bankruptcy in the thirties, World War II and the Japanese Occupation of Singapore in the forties, the flirtation with modernism in the fifties, stiff competition from the new international-style hotels built along Orchard Road in the sixties and seventies, and plans to demolish the old buildings and replace them with a skyscraper in the early eighties, Raffles Hotel now faced the biggest threat of all: creaking old age. The Grand Old Lady was desperately in need, not just of a facelift, but of major surgery if she was going to survive into her second century. Her centenary came and went, she was gazetted a National Monument and, finally, in 1989 plans to carefully restore the hotel were unveiled.

Today Raffles Hotel bears little resemblance to what she was a decade ago. Instead she resembles her earlier self — a grand Oriental hotel, the hotel that 'stands for all the fables of the Exotic East' as Somerset Maugham so wonderfully described it. Which brings us to the third element of Raffles style: a quintessentially Singaporean blend of old and new, East and West, heritage and high tech. The hotel is now infused with life in a manner that honours its past and traditions as much as it suits the present. The quality of timelessness is evident throughout the hotel: in the lush gardens, generously proportioned rooms and spacious suites, the fine restaurants, the famous Long Bar, the shady verandahs, the polished timber floors and the whirring ceiling fans.

Because of the scale of the restoration, Raffles closed its doors to travellers for the very first time. The selection of 1915 as the benchmark year for restoration rendered many potentially difficult decisions straightforward. The twenties ballroom was removed while its 1913-1919 predecessor, a cast-iron portico, was faithfully reconstructed. The building at the corner of Bras Basah Road and Beach Road was returned to its previous incarnation as the Bar and Billiard Room. Old photographs, picture

postcards, original building plans and physical evidence were tracked down and scrutinized in order to restore the buildings as authentically as possible.

Few pieces of original furniture had survived. Several teak desks were rescued from staff quarters, refinished and are now found in the suites. A larger grouping of teak tables and chairs are now in the Bar and Billiard Room along with two antique billiard tables, one original to Raffles, the other from the former residence of the colonial governor. Pride of place in the lobby is given to the grandfather clock, believed to be the oldest surviving piece of the Sarkies' furniture.

Among the many antiques specially purchased for the hotel were antique desks from China and Southeast Asia. All of the antiques were sourced from Singapore with some coming from now demolished bungalows.

Many additional antiques had to be sourced, especially for the Main Building which is the heart of the hotel and its face to the world. Today the Main Building houses the lobby and reception desk, the Writers' Bar, two historic restaurants, Raffles Grill and the Tiffin Room, the eight premier Grand Hotel Suites and two large Drawing Rooms for the use of hotel residents. The sourcing of the antiques was deliberately accomplished in Singapore over a two-year period. The hotel's eclectic collection reflects Singapore's multi-ethnicity and its traditional role as emporium of the East and meeting place of East and West.

Several pieces have unusual provenance. An enormous teak dining table, set of chairs and sideboard from the now-demolished home of a prominent Chinese family found a new home in the Sir Stamford Raffles Suite alongside original nineteenth century engravings of Singapore. A pair of deep reclining chairs from the bedroom suites of Eu Villa, the extravagant mansion built by millionaire Eu Tong Sen in the twenties, were acquired and placed, one each, in the master bedrooms of the Sarkies and Sir Stamford Raffles Suites. A large Victorian cast-iron fountain, shipped out to Singapore from Glasgow over a century ago was rescued from oblivion, restored, and is now installed in the Palm Garden.

Others pieces came via dealers from old Singapore homes unknown. One prized find is an opium bed stashed away for years by a local dealer, its remarkable carvings display a rare medley of tropical flora and birds. Equally important are the elaborate Victorian sideboards in teak carved in Singapore for wealthy Peranakan families whose aesthetic tastes were a richly eclectic blending of Chinese, English and Malay elements. Then there are the imported pieces: European-style dressers in Chinese hardwoods carved around the turn of the century in Shanghai; blackwood library tables made to European tastes in Indochina; traditional Chinese writing desks; and colonial-style teak chairs and tables.

To complement the antique furniture, an important collection of nineteenth century engravings and photographs of Singapore and Southeast Asia was acquired. The engravings include rare early views of the Singapore River, delightful botanicals as well as stunning topographical views. The photographs were originally produced for travellers by professional firms in the days before easy amateur photography and picture postcards. Reproductions of these remarkable views are found in the suites, giving guests an instant impression of what Singapore was like when Raffles was in its early heyday.

An extensive and valuable collection of over 700 Oriental carpets was acquired for the restaurants, suites and public areas. The centrepiece of the collection is an exceptionally large, richly coloured carpet which takes pride of place in the lobby and was woven by hand in the studio of the talented master carpetmaker Saber, in Persia between 1930 and 1935. Complementing it are two other carpets, also handcrafted by Saber in the thirties when he was at the height of his fame.

As the reopening date approached, the pace quickened: craftsmen fussed over the hotel, giving her the final buff and polish. By 16 September 1991 the noble proportions of the hotel's façade were complete and welcoming once more. Sikh doormen stood immaculate in their new Gieves & Hawkes uniforms under the restored cast-iron portico. In the lobby the Carrara marble floor was polished to shining perfection, the Oriental carpets in place, the flowers fresh, fragrant, colourful and abundant. The doors were opened at precisely 10 a.m.

On the pages that follow you will see the spaces and proportions, the antiques and artwork, the luxurious textures and details, that together compose Raffles Hotel style. What is impossible to convey in photographs is its fourth and final element: the personalised service provided by discreet and well-trained staff. With only 104 suites, Raffles Hotel is not unlike a stately home where guests are treated as residents and pampered in an atmosphere of privacy and intimacy. From Executive Director Richard Helfer and General Manager Jennie Chua to the doormen, room valets, restaurant captains and flower girls — everyone conspires to make a stay in Raffles a truly unforgettable experience. As one recent guest wrote of her stay, 'I think I've died and gone to hotel heaven. Thank you for your exquisite care.' Since Raffles re-emergence from renovation it has twice been voted the world's leading independent hotel.

The best way to enjoy Raffles Hotel style is, of course, to stay in the hotel. The Shanghai jars are no more. Gone, too, is the splendid Conradesque seaview that was so much a part of the hotel's early character. It has been many decades since a tiger visited the Bar and Billiard Room or a python was found hiding among the potted plants on the verandah. But as you sit as dusk falls on one of the hotel's splendid verandahs, preferably with a cool Singapore Sling in hand, and listen carefully, you can still hear the creaking floorboards, the wind through the Traveller's palms and the century of secrets Raffles Hotel carries within her walls.

Champagne, complete with personalised buckets, has always been an essential part of Raffles Hotel style.

***Following pages**: The façade of the main building has been restored to its circa 1915 appearance.*

Tropical Splendour

In the context of today's architectural trends Raffles Hotel is remarkably understated and unobtrusive. No polished chrome, high-tech claddings or glitzy glass here. Much of the hotel is protected by trees, ferns and flowering plants, the red tiled roofs of the two and three storey buildings, the terracotta-tiled courtyards and simple white walls a satisfying contrast to the lush greenery. The strongest statement is the dazzling white façade of the Main Building with its confident and pleasing interpretation of classicism. Although perhaps somewhat quaint in relationship to its high-rise neighbours, the Main Building continues to hold its own in the urban landscape.

The opening of the Main Building in 1899 was a benchmark both in terms of architecture and in standards of hotel comfort. The style of architecture, described at the time as 'Renaissance in appearance' was the absolute height of fashion. The electrical system, powered by the hotel's own generator, was one of the first on the island and powered ceiling fans, service bells and electric lights, all of which improved the comfort of guests enormously. Such innovations were not, however, universally welcome and the unaccustomed blaze of lights came under particular attack. Still, the opening of the Main Building secured Raffles' position as the 'finest Caravanserai east of Suez'.

Another benchmark was the hotel's recent restoration. For the first time ever Raffles Hotel closed its doors completely as the creaking old buildings were lovingly restored. Between 1899 and 1989 any number of architectural additions and amendments had been introduced in an *ad hoc* manner. The restoration enabled the buildings to be returned to their circa-1915 heyday. Columns, capitals and timber floors were renewed while bathrooms installed on verandahs were happily relocated. Essential modern services were thoroughly upgraded and carefully imbedded in the building fabric. The grand timber staircase and cast-iron front portico, both of which had disappeared, were faithfully rebuilt according to original architectural plans.

Equally important was the attention lavished on the gardens. Existing mature palms and frangipani trees, which have long formed the backbone of the gardens, were zealously guarded. On the newly acquired adjacent land, where the hotel's arcade was built, new gardens were lovingly planted. Today the Fern Court, Palm Garden, Raffles Courtyard and The Lawn are as admired as the far older Palm Court. The Palm Garden is home to a large cast-iron fountain with sprouting dolphins transported from Glasgow to Singapore over a hundred years ago and derelict for decades. Here also are several casuarina trees planted in honour of Somerset Maugham who called his first book of short stories set in the East, published in 1926, *The Casuarina Tree*. Maugham explained the title thus: the casuarina is a grey, rugged tree found on tropical coasts, a bit grim beside the lush vegetation about it and suggesting exiled Europeans who in temperament and stamina were often ill-equipped for life in the Tropics.

Early morning on the front verandah (opposite, below and following pages). With its vast height, cool Carrara marble floor and brass light fixtures, the front verandah conjures up memories of an earlier era — and admirably serves as an efficient arrival porch for today's vehicles.

The Palm Court and the Main Building. Perhaps the most famous of the hotel's gardens, and the most historic, the Palm Court dates back to the late nineteenth century when an L-shaped wing enclosed the space. By the seventies, however, it had become cluttered and overcrowded with a swimming pool and alfresco dining. Now returned to a tranquil private residential expanse, it resembles postcard views of the twenties. Most of the 14-metre tall Livistona rotundifolia palms are originals and were carefully protected during the restoration, as were the garden's frangipani trees (Plumeria rubra and Plumeria alba). The gravel path (above) echoes the hotel's gravel-paved elliptical front drive; the sound of the river stone crunching underfoot, or under wheel, adds an aural dimension to Raffles. The graceful porch (following pages) is reminiscent of traditional nineteenth-century Singapore bungalow design; the original plan for the first such structure at the hotel is dated 1890.

Verandahs. In the nineteenth century verandahs were an essential feature of gracious living — and an important buffer zone between the glare of the sun drenched outdoors and the dimness of interiors. Indeed, most of Raffles Hotel's buildings were designed with both front and back verandahs. The back verandahs were strictly utilitarian and were used by servants to deliver water and remove night soil. Over time many verandahs were enclosed, turned into toilets or converted into airconditioned rooms. Today, all the verandahs, front (above) and back (right), have been restored. Especially grandiose are the deep Main Building verandahs (opposite) with their timber floors and tall connecting French doors. The lights were specially created by marrying various parts from old light fixtures found in local antique shops.

Raffles Hotel's beautiful gardens contain over 50,000 plants — 80 different species in all — cared for by the hotel's own horticulturist and a staff of six full-time gardeners. While the gardens boast several rare species, such as the Heliconia 'Black Magic' recently planted in the Palm Garden, most are durable and well-known tropical varieties. Indeed, the backbone of the garden consists of three particular species associated with Raffles since its earliest days: the tall, dignified Livistona palm, the ever-beguiling Traveller's palm (Ravenala madagascariensis) and the fragrant, romantic frangipani tree with its perfect yellow and white flowers. The gardens also act as an important cushion between the hotel and the city. Along Beach Road (right) the planting includes the colourful Peacock flower (Caesalpinia pulcherrima).

Continuity amidst a changing city. Thanks to the acquisition of adjacent land, the hotel's gardens are now considerably larger and cover nearly a quarter of Raffles' land area. Raffles Courtyard (left) is a large outdoor dining area with cast-iron pavilions and a porch that replicates the Sarkies' original Palm Court design. The ubiquitous and shady Traveller's palm (usually found with a smaller palm regenerating beneath it) can be contemplated from many vantage points, including the rattan tables and chairs found outside each of the suites (opposite). Equally picturesque are the Fiji palms (Pritchardia pacifica) above.

Previous pages: The lush and jungle-like Fern Court. Species found in the court include breadfruit trees (Artocarpus altilis), *torch ginger* (Nicolaia speciosa), *bird's nest ferns* (Asplenium nidus), *tree ferns* (Cyathea arborea) *and lady's palms* (Rhapis excelsa).

These pages: A number of flowering plants add colour and texture to the gardens including heliconia (top left), red ginger (top right) and the yellow and white frangipani (right). A small jungle-like courtyard (opposite) is located in Raffles Hotel Arcade outside the Lady Sophia Suite, a small function room named in honour of the wife of Sir Stamford Raffles who established modern Singapore in 1819. Raffles was a keen botanist and founded Singapore's first Botanic Gardens (1822). Plantings include coconut trees and bamboo. The large leafy plant in the foreground is Alocasia odora.

Sweeping verandahs are also an architectural feature of Raffles Hotel Arcade. Here are located restaurants, shops, the hotel's museum as well as Jubilee Hall, a cosy theatre, and the Ballroom (left). The vistas are charmingly enlivened by whimsical trompe l'oeil murals executed by the San Francisco artist Carlos Marchiori whose first visit to Raffles Hotel produced a series of opulent murals in the Ballroom, including one into which the hotel is painted (above).

Following pages: This cast-iron fountain was imported from Glasgow around 1890. A landmark on Orchard Road until it disappeared from public view, it was found in pieces in the garden of a Singapore family who donated it to the hotel.

37

CHAPTER 3

In Residence

Discreet luxury, abundant comforts, attentive but unobtrusive service. These are the magical ingredients that distinguish a truly great hotel anywhere in the world; the interpretation of these ingredients is what infuses a great hotel with its own unique style.

At Raffles the mood is immediately established by the sound of crunching pebbles as the taxi (preferably one of the hotel's own burgundy-coloured London taxis fitted out with cream leather seats and Oriental carpets) navigates the elliptical gravel-covered front drive, and by the dignified doormen who welcome each guest as if he or she were returning home. The anticipation is heightened as, leaving behind the heat and glare of the tropical sun, one enters the deliciously cool light-filled lobby with its soaring atrium, Persian carpets, fresh flowers, Carrara marble floors, comfortable furniture, and wonderfully timeless 'Crossroads of the East' atmosphere.

Peculiar to Raffles are the enormous Drawing Rooms above the lobby. These are for hotel residents and were conceived and built at a time when the comfort of cooler open spaces was preferable to bedrooms for reading and relaxation. Times have, of course, changed and so have social habits but the Drawing Rooms survive and are once again filled with fine antiques, reading lamps and periodicals far more recent than guests were once accustomed to.

But it is in the 104 suites that one experiences most intimately the many features that compose the hotel's style, whether in the elegant Grand Hotel Suites, the evocative Personality Suites named after well known writers and other famous visitors, the Raffles Inc. State Rooms designed to accommodate business travellers or in any of the typical suites — all of which are dispersed over five wings buffered by tropical gardens and courtyards linked by verandahs.

Here Raffles style is expressed in both the visible and invisible: in the thoughtful details of the interiors and the little luxuries such as the Oriental carpets, antiques and engravings; in delicious comforts such as the spacious bathrooms and wardrobes, the stack of thick white bath towels and the monogrammed linens; in the tactful service of the room valets and their ability to make guests feel completely relaxed, and in the unexpected such as the fable of the East placed on the pillow each evening for bedtime reading.

If there is one common factor which unifies all of these various and diverse elements it is the seamless combination of the modern and the traditional. Raffles Hotel is, after all, many things to many people. International landmark, grand historic hotel, glittering social venue, the hotel must effortlessly accommodate travellers as diverse as romantics in search of the luminous spirit of Somerset Maugham and fast-track executives far more concerned with efficiency, service and the gym than heritage. Whatever the challenge may be in creating a perfect home away from home for its guests and residents, Raffles Hotel prides itself in rising to the occasion in its own inimitable way each and every time.

Raffles' interiors combine luxurious Oriental antiques and decorative touches with comfortable European-style furniture and artwork. The living room of the Sir Stamford Raffles Suite (opposite) juxtaposes an English reading chair and foot stool with an unusual Peranakan screen with gilt trim that once graced an old Singapore home. The English floral painting (above) is one of a large pair which hang outside the Tiffin Room.

Gracious, airy and elegant, the lobby (opposite) is the very heart of Raffles Hotel. Respectfully restored to its original splendour, this huge space is a lesson in tropical architecture. The absence of internal walls around the central atrium, which culminates in a light-giving clerestory, ensured maximum air circulation. The ground floor was designed to impress as the Main Dining Room. Dining is still part of the Raffles tradition here in the Tiffin Room and Raffles Grill, the two restaurants which flank the lobby. The early twentieth century circular table in the foreground was made in Vietnam to a French design. The vase is Chinese porcelain. The historic clock (above and right) is the oldest surviving piece of hotel furniture and can be found between the front doors. It stands eight feet tall. The clock's movement was made by S. Smith & Son, Clerkenwell, London, between 1835 and 1842. The plaque of the lobby safe (right) has been polished smooth since 1857.

The bartender of the Writers' Bar (left) mixes drinks under the watchful eyes of some of the famous authors associated with the hotel including Joseph Conrad, Rudyard Kipling, Somerset Maugham and Noel Coward. Kipling was an early visitor (1889) who advised travellers to 'Feed at Raffles . . . .' More than half a century later Somerset Maugham declared that Raffles Hotel 'stands for all the fables of the exotic East'. The upper floors of the Main Building house the eight evocatively named premier Grand Hotel Suites — Sir Stamford Raffles Suite, Sarkies Suite, Straits Settlements Suite, Hotel de l'Europe Suite as well as the Batavia, Temasak, Cathay and Golden Chersonese Suites.

The suites can be reached either by elevator or via the magnificent dark timber staircase (above) which, having been removed years ago, has been faithfully recreated from the original building plans. Oriental pots (right) filled with yellow cane palms soften the voluminous spaces of the Main Building Drawing Rooms.

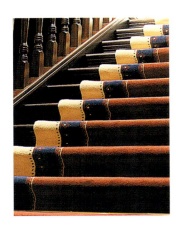

Spacious Drawing Rooms
are found on the second
and third levels of the
Main Building. Here long
ago residents once passed
away their waking hours
(bedrooms were just for
sleeping) writing letters,
reading the European
newspapers (several weeks
late) or socialising with
fellow guests. Today the
rooms are once again
comfortably appointed
with chairs, lamps and, of
course, far more current
periodicals. The marble-
top table is early twentieth
century Vietnamese
French colonial.

'This is really an apology for staying on eight days longer than originally requested. We were enjoying ourselves so much we simply couldn't leave,' penned a recent guest to the General Manager. Twice voted the world's leading independent hotel since its reopening, Raffles never fails to calm and inspire residents with its unusual qualities and spaces. In this Drawing Room (opposite) the serene composition includes Oriental carpets, blue-and-white Chinese porcelain pots, small Chinese blackwood tables and a pair of larger marble-top teak consuls in the Peranakan style (right). Early morning sunshine pours through the fanlight (above) casting a seductive shadow. The sun shading device is in the form of French coloured glass fanlights and windows, the colour and pattern of which is based on a fragment of glass found buried above a false ceiling and uncovered during restoration work.

The Sir Stamford Raffles Suite is named after the East India Company official who founded the modern port of Singapore in 1819 and is the hotel's namesake. The suite was designed to recreate the feeling of a spacious old colonial bungalow and indeed the architecture of the space is so strong a decorative feature that little is required in the way of additional adornment.

The living room windows overlook the Palm Court and front drive of the hotel. The living room features a French colonial library table and Chinese desk chair. The coffee table is early twentieth century Chinese-Annamese and is finely inlaid with mother-of pearl scenes (above). An original engraving of Sir Stamford Raffles' bust (left) dated 1824 hangs in the living room.

Previous pages: The dining room of the Sir Stamford Raffles Suite features two wonderful colonial sideboards. The large teak sideboard on the left is from a circa 1913 Singapore home and was obtained days before the opening of the restored hotel. It is part of a suite that included the dining table and chairs now in the Sarkies Suite (see page 56). The set of Javanese engravings on the wall are from Sir Stamford Raffles' scholarly History of Java, published in London in 1870. The dining room has its own set of Tiffany & Co. Shell and Thread *silver flatware with matching china. The dining room is connected by a small vestibule to two bedrooms.* **These pages:** *The dressing table in the second bedroom (above) was made in Shanghai in the twenties. The master bedroom (right) is fit for a king, the coronas adding a regal touch.*

The Sarkies Suite is named in honour of the enterprising Armenian family who established Raffles Hotel in 1887 and ran it until the early thirties. The large dining table (above) in the suite's private dining room is part of a set of furniture which features hand-forged brass fittings. The table was designed to cater for both Chinese and Western dining as the oval tabletop converts into a circle when several of the leaves are removed. Reflected in the dining room's elaborate English colonial teak sideboard (opposite) is the suite's living room, a composition of comfortable furniture and Oriental antiques. For formal entertaining the suite has its own set of Tiffany & Co. Audubon silver flatware and matching china.

More views of the Sarkies Suite. An early twentieth century photograph of the Sarkies brothers (left) hangs in the entrance. The master bedroom includes an enormous Chinese blackwood cupboard (above) with Gothic touches made by Shanghainese craftsmen in a European style around the turn of the century. The lounge chair partially visible on the right is from Eu Villa, the famous mansion built by a well-known Chinese businessman in the twenties. A small vestibule (right) connects the two bedrooms to the verandah and the rest of the suite. The half doors, or pintu pagar, are from one of Singapore's old seaside bungalows and were acquired days before the house was demolished. The suite also contains two early twentieth century Cantonese blackwood recliners.

More views of the Grand
Hotel Suites. The Hotel de
l'Europe Suite is named in
honour of Raffles Hotel's
main rival until the
thirties. Among its
antiques are an unusual
Art Deco dressing table
probably made in
Shanghai in the twenties
(opposite), an early
twentieth century Chinese
desk in blackwood (above)
and a Straits Settlement-
style teak umbrella stand
(left). The Cathay Suite
(following pages) also
features a Chinese
blackwood desk and is
the perfect place to pen
a letter or postcard home.
The wardrobe has lacquer
panels handsomely
painted in gold.

61

One of the most unexpectedly charming corners of the hotel is the two storey lounge linked by a handsome timber staircase in the Bras Basah Wing. Opened in 1904, the three storey wing was actually designed as a home away from home for longer term hotel guests. It also had one of the town's first shopping arcades on the ground floor. At the heart of this wing is the lounge which now serves residents of Raffles Inc., the hotel's business address. The second floor is furnished with comfortable rattan chairs, a writing desk, paintings by Singapore artists and lots of reading materials.

More views of the Raffles Inc. lounge. The furnishings were carefully selected to create a residential atmosphere. The colonial style teak library table is from an old Singapore house. The large painting over the sofa is of the old shophouses of nearby Seah Street and is by Singapore artist Chua Eck Kay.

Suite 102, the Somerset Maugham Suite, is one of the hotel's most popular suites. It overlooks the Palm Court and is the room Maugham requested on his many visits to the hotel. During his last visit, in 1960, he was photographed talking to a fan in the suite (far left) which had been decidedly 'modernised' with plaid fabrics and aluminium lamps. Today the furnishings are more in keeping with Maugham's earlier visits in the twenties. The desk is English colonial and memorabilia includes an original autographed photograph of Maugham, books and a facsimile of a thank-you letter written to and donated by former Raffles Hotel Manager Franz Schutzman.

The Charlie Chaplin Suite. Chaplin was one of the world's new royalty — the kings and queens of Hollywood — hosted by Raffles in the twenties and thirties. During his first visit in 1932 he was photographed having a meal in the Dining Room with his brother (left). The view (above) of the suite peaks through the front door into the living room and the spacious bedroom beyond. The dainty Chinese desk at the far end is Shanghainese blackwood. Above it hangs a small collection of Chaplin memorabilia. Other personality suites have been named after photographer John Thomson, writer Joseph Conrad, the multi-talented Noel Coward, actress Ava Gardener and, most recently, after the Chilean poet Pablo Neruda.

CHAPTER 4

Prized Possessions

No grand hotel is complete without a treasure trove of fine antiques and artwork. Raffles Hotel is no exception. Oriental carpets, handpicked for the public areas and suites; an array of Oriental antiques, in teak from Singapore and the old Straits Settlements or in the hardwoods of Vietnam and China, elaborately carved and reflecting a century of cross-cultural influences, from elaborate Victorian and Peranakan-style sideboards and Art Deco dressing tables to Chinese scholars' desks and impressive opium beds; rare nineteenth-century engravings of Singapore made when the town ran barely a mile from the shore and tigers still wandered out of the jungle and onto the streets; and early photographs of the island, views produced by commercial firms mainly for sale to tourists, their beautiful sepia tones and artful compositions now appreciated for their artistic expression as well as for their historical significance, brilliantly informing us of the island's transformation from an isolated settlement of the British East India Company to a strategic British colony, port city and all-important crossroads of the East.

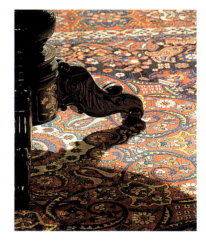

And all lovingly acquired to grace Raffles renewed.

Then there are the pieces with unusual provenance. Several of the pieces were discovered at just the right moment, as if destined to find a new home in Raffles Hotel. The most spectacular of these 'finds' is a large teak dining table with its chairs and two magnificent sideboards. Just days before the hotel's reopening in September of 1991, with nearly all the furniture in place, a phone call from a thoughtful supporter who had danced at Raffles before World War II led to their acquisition. How appropriate they are in both scale and style for the suites they grace.

Very few of Raffles' older furnishings have survived. The handsome grandfather clock that stands sentinel in the lobby is perhaps the oldest, although the casing is Art Deco in style and much later than the English clockworks. There are a number of teak desks scattered throughout the suites, small brass plaques acknowledging their origins. One of the billiard tables in the Bar and Billiard Room is believed to be original (the other, equally old, came, via a circuitous route, from what was once Government House and the home of the colonial governor and is now the Istana and the official home of the President of Singapore). Much of the furniture in the Bar and Billiard Room originated in the Singapore Town Club but found a home on Raffles' verandahs several decades ago, the chance acquisition of an old photograph of the club's dining room revealing their origins.

The carpets, antiques and artwork add depth, interest and character to interiors conceived primarily for comfort. Each piece may be quietly appreciated in its own right or within the context of its surroundings. Nothing is contrived, and the subdued elegance, together with the warm hospitality of the staff, creates an atmosphere conducive to quiet relaxation as well as sophisticated conviviality.

The hotel's collection of some 700 Oriental carpets was amassed over a two-year period and includes the primitive Oriental rugs of nomads as well as sophisticated carpets intended for a city market. One very special piece is this beautifully mellowed turn-of-the-century Persian Bakhtiar (above). The centrepiece of the collection is an exceptionally large, richly hued masterpiece (opposite) woven by hand in the studio of the gifted master carpetmaker Saber, in Persia, between 1930 and 1935.

A wealth of colours and shades. In the living room of the Sarkies Suite (opposite) is a large carpet remarkable for its subdued, elegant colours and beautiful patina. It was made in the early years of the century and was specially bought for the suite in the city of Meshed in northeast Iran.

The design is similar to the famous Ardebil rug in the Victoria and Albert Museum in London and is referred to as the 'Sheikh Safi' design. The carpets are a much admired element of Raffles Hotel style. Each suite has between four and five carpets, each displaying intense colours and patterns.

Among the antiques sourced during the restoration are two teak pieces in *Raffles Grill*. The rather grand umbrella stand (above) once graced the front hall of a large Singapore Peranakan home and reflects turn-of-the-century Peranakan style with its eclectic blend of Chinese, English Victorian and Malay elements. The porcelain tiles (above and left), however, are hotel originals and were among the few intact decorative pieces rescued during the restoration. The elaborate Victorian cupboard (right) was made in the Straits Settlements and may have once graced the dining room of a rubber planter's home.

Two spectacular opium beds near the main staircase reveal the consummate skill of Chinese carvers around the turn of the century. One of the beds (right and opposite) was acquired by a local antique dealer from a Singapore residence on the east coast of the island and is unusual in that it features exquisitely executed tropical motifs including banana leaves and birds. Equally fine is the workmanship of an opium bed originally from Vietnam (above) where the curvaceous, almost flirtatious, workmanship shows a strong French colonial influence.

The astounding skill and imagination of the humble carpenter is displayed in numerous antique pieces within the walls and corridors of Raffles. Feline themes abound: in the curvaceous base of the Vietnamese blackwood table (above), the diminutive mythical animals upon which a classic Peranakan cupboard rests (this page, far left) and on an astonishingly elaborate Chinese altar table (left).

The ornate Victorian piano (opposite) in one of the Main Building's Drawing Rooms was manufactured by Eungblut & Eungblut of London for one J. Gregory, 27 Lister Gate, Nottingham, England. Music has long been a special aspect of Raffles style — from the specially composed Raffles March and big band sound of the Raffles Orchestra of the twenties and thirties, to Noel Coward's nostalgic, witty songs.

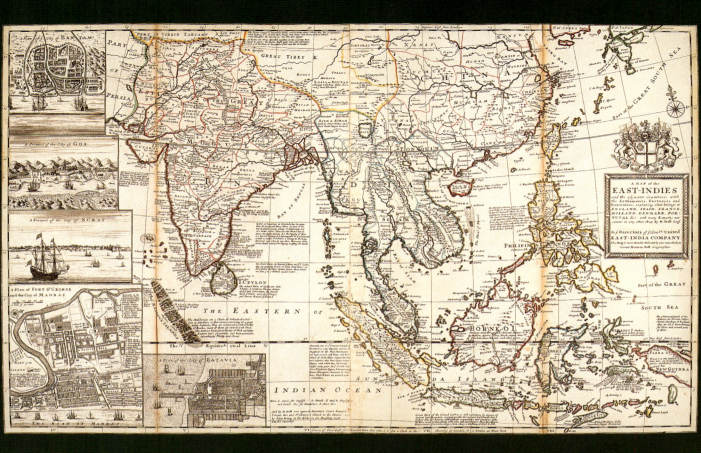

SINGAPORE.

Art treasures from the
Raffles Hotel collection.
The Map of the East
Indies and the Adjacent
Countries with the
Settlements, Factories and
Territories explaining
what belongs to England,
Spain, France, Holland,
Denmark and Portugal
(opposite, top) was made
by geographer Herman
Moll, active from 1678 to
1732, for the directors of
the East India Company.
The largest and most
spectacular engraving of
old Singapore in the hotel's
collection is Singapore
from Mount Wallich at
Sunrise (opposite, bottom)
based on a painting by
Percy Carpenter, published
in London in 1858. A rare
original engraving is in
the hotel's museum.
Hanging in the Hotel de
l'Europe Suite (above and
left) is an evocative scene
that captures the early
days of the so-called
'Golden Age of Travel'.
Entitled For the Shore it
was published in The
Graphic, in London,
in 1883.

Dessiné par Geupil. Lithᵗᵉ par Eugᵉ Cicéri.   Gide Éditeur.   Lith. de Thierry frères Paris.

RADE ET VILLE DE SINCAPOUR

(Vue Générale.)

Dessiné par Lebreton. Lith. par Sabatier. fig. par Bayot.   Gide Éditeur.   Imp. par Lemercier.

RADE DE SINCAPOUR

prise de la maison du Gouverneur.

(Malaisie.)

SINGAPORE.

R.E del. et lith.

Printed by Hullmandel & Walton

London: Hurst & Blackett, Great Marlborough Street

Rare engravings of old Singapore hang throughout the Main Building. The charming view of the seafront and Beach Road (above) from 1850 was based on a sketch by the artist Robert Elwes and published in his book A Sketcher's Tour Around the World in London in 1854; the old banyan tree was a *Singapore landmark until it was destroyed by a fire about 1875. The two French prints (left) were published in Paris in an Atlas Pittoresque that recorded the 1837-1840 voyage of exploration led by Dumont D'Urville. Another French expedition of the 1830s produced the so-called Bonite prints (following pages),* *La Bonite being the name of the vessel. It spent five days in Singapore in 1837. The woodblock prints of Malacca's Chinatown and a Malay village scene (pages 88 and 89) are the work of American artist Elizabeth Keith who travelled extensively in Asia in the twenties and thirties and they hang in Doc Cheng's restaurant.*

Dessiné par Lauvergne.　　　Im Lemercier Bernard et C.	　Lith par Bichebois Fig par Adam

ENVIRONS DE SINCAPOUR

ENVIRONS DE SINCAPOUR

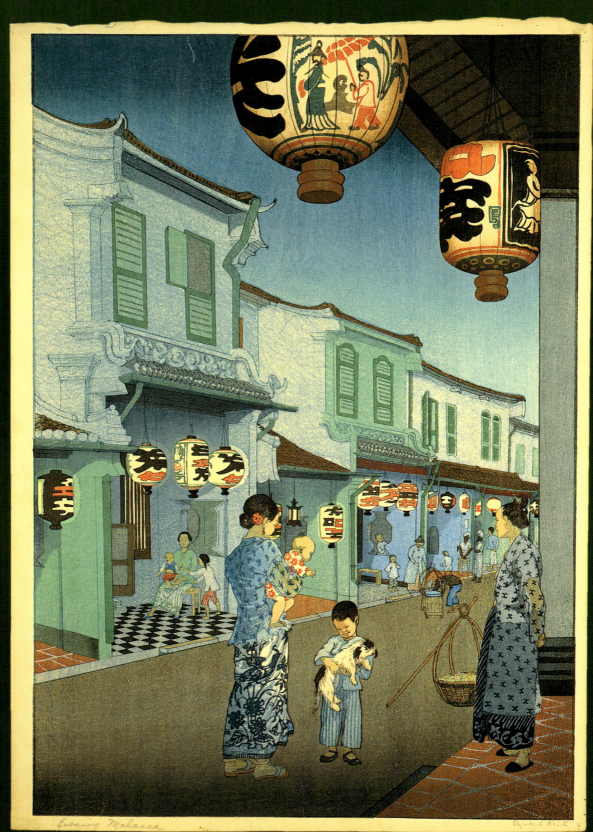

Evening Malacca   Elizabeth Keith

Night scene Malacca   Elizabeth Keith

200-Raffles Hotel

Scenery at the Harbour. S. pore. 4

1232-Commercial Square

The hotel's collection of original nineteenth-century photographs of Singapore and Southeast Asia is extensive; reproductions hang in all of the typical suites. These images were produced throughout the East by commercial studios in port cities specifically to cater to the needs of travellers who collected them as souvenirs in the days before easy amateur photography.

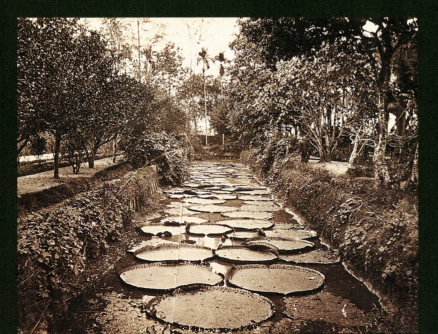

The clarity of detail, whether of tropical fruit in the studio or Raffles Hotel itself (previous pages), town and port scenes (opposite page and following pages) or nature (left and following pages) belie the inherent difficulties of undertaking early photography in the tropics. Such images are a captivating record of Singapore during the years Raffles Hotel achieved its early fame.

CHAPTER 5

Time for Tea

There are many ways to enjoy a visit to Raffles Hotel, but dining surely ranks amongst the most satisfying and memorable of experiences. Each of the hotel's restaurants serves a cuisine that is unique: from the continental classics of Raffles Grill to the Southeast Asian and Anglo-Indian curries of the Tiffin Room; from the traditional Cantonese flavours of the Empress Room to the robust tastes of the Singaporean hawker food in the Empire Cafe and the East-West Fusion Cuisine of the award-winning Doc Cheng's. Even the hearty sandwiches served up at the Seah Street Deli have that special Raffles touch.

The tradition of culinary excellence is an old one, stretching back to the hotel's earliest days. The first accolade was bestowed by Rudyard Kipling who stopped in Singapore in 1889, 'Providence conducted me along a beach, in full view of five miles of shipping — five solid miles of masts and funnels — to a place called Raffles Hotel where the food is as excellent as the rooms are bad'. (Mind you, Kipling visited the modest hostelry before the Sarkies worked their magic.) The author so enjoyed his meal that, after a visit to the Botanic Gardens, he crept back in order to 'eat six different chutneys with one curry.'

The commitment to culinary excellence was further reinforced with the completion of the Main Building where the entire ground floor was originally occupied by an enormous dining room 'capable of seating 500 persons'. This was a space designed to impress. And it did. 'Admittedly the most spacious and beautiful public banquet hall in Asia,' reported the local press. Not long after, new kitchens were built and two French chefs were recruited.

The hotel's recent renewal opened a new and exciting chapter in Raffles' culinary story. Several long established traditions continue (the Tiffin Room offers at least six different chutneys with curry), others have been revived and, in keeping with changed lifestyles and trends, new ones have been added. Thus dining at Raffles Hotel embraces many elements: the freshest of ingredients, the uncommon artistry of talented chefs, attentive yet unobtrusive service, and, of course, the perfection of the table settings and the food presentation, whether it is the lofty *foie gras* served on Tiffany & Co. china and eaten with matching silver flatware in the elegant surroundings of the private dining room of the Sir Stamford Raffles or Sarkies suites or the humble roti prata served on a banana leaf and eaten by hand in the Empire Cafe. Given such diversity it is no small challenge for the staff to ensure that each and every meal served is a memorable event.

Finally, no chapter on dining at Raffles Hotel would be complete without a mention of the hotel's famed bars — the Bar and Billiard Room, which also serves up a marvellous buffet lunch and afternoon high tea, the famous Writers' Bar in the lobby and, last but not least, the historic Long Bar where visitors still celebrate one of the most important rites of passage of world travel: imbibing a Singapore Sling.

Dining at Raffles has always been a memorable experience. Today each of the hotel's eight restaurants serves a cuisine that is a unique culinary tradition unto itself. One of the most popular, and historic, restaurants is the Tiffin Room (opposite) seen here from the Palm Garden through the Tiffin Room's tall French doors. The chairs in the photograph above, of dining at the Town Club circa 1915, were bought by the hotel years ago and are now in the Bar and Billiard Room.

The Tiffin Room. Tiffin, properly defined as a light mid-day meal, has long been a Raffles tradition. For most of this century a mild chicken curry was one of the few Asian mainstays on the hotel's daily menu as the partaking of Sunday tiffin curry was an essential aspect of colonial life. Today's tiffin buffet can be enjoyed for lunch or dinner in an authentic atmosphere. The designs of the tables, chairs, and uniforms are all based on early photographs. The brisk, white-jacketed waiters wear badges (right) which replicate a prewar tukang ayer, or 'water carrier' badge, while the silver vase and salt and pepper shakers (opposite) are replicas of decades-old silver plate pieces discovered in a storeroom during the restoration.

TIFFIN ROOM

The Raffles Tiffin Rooms
was opened in 1892 and run by the
Sarkies brothers in Commercial Square,
now known as Raffles Place.
It was a grand and popular restaurant
which could seat up to 200 people,
with punkahs to keep the place cool.
When the restaurant closed down
around 1910, the hotel carried on
the tradition of serving
Tiffin Curry at the Dining Room, which became known as
the Tiffin Room.

The private dining room of the Tiffin Room (above) features a series of sketches (left) of the hotel's restoration by Sir Hugh Casson, the English architect and artist who made a special visit to Singapore and Raffles shortly after restoration work commenced.

The award-winning Doc Cheng's (above). Few restaurants celebrate the fusion of East-West cuisines with more dazzle and flair. The contemporary Chinese painting is by mainland artist Zhu Wei.

Dining in style. Elegant and formal, Raffles Grill (right) looks much as it did when the management first invited diners to 'book tables early to avoid disappointment'. With its classical architectural details beautifully

restored, the carefully chosen antiques and the enormous French windows overlooking the verandah and Palm Court, the room conveys a sense of timeless grace. Here the traditional art of gracious hospitality has been perfected.

The Empress Room. The decoration of Raffles Hotel's fine Cantonese restaurant was inspired by traditional Chinese domestic architecture and is welcoming, calming and deliberately residential, with terracotta tiled floors, old fashioned lace curtains, timber panels and ceiling, and simple white china and blackwood chopsticks set on peach tablecloths. A series of Chinese paintings in the entrance waiting area (left) feature the Eight Immortals. In the private dining room are several 'beautiful lady' or Meinu Yuefenpai calendar posters (above). Produced in Shanghai in the twenties and thirties as advertisements, the posters are representative of China's earliest commercial art. The elegant figures are portrayed with remarkable sophistication and great attention to detail.

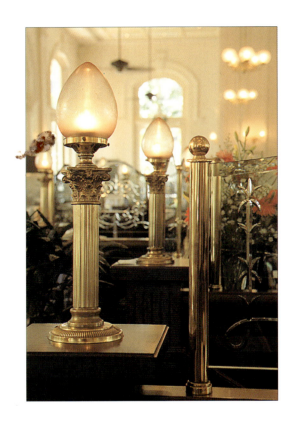

The Bar and Billiard Room harks back to the days when billiard tables were as common in a hotel as a swimming pool is today. The structure, which straddles the corner of Beach and Bras Basah Roads has seen numerous renovations. Today it resembles the circa 1907-1917 Bar and Billiard Room, cast-iron portico and all. Over three-quarters of the furniture, mostly in teak, is original to the hotel. Previously scattered throughout the verandahs and rooms, the furniture was catalogued, restored, and relocated here. A small brass plaque identifies each piece. There are two antique billiard tables, one is a Raffles Hotel original while the other graced Government House (now the Istana) and was the colonial governor's billiard table. Legend has it that during the Japanese bombing of Singapore the wife of Governor Sir Shenton Thomas sought refuge under the table and was remarkably well protected when the table suffered a shattering crack.

The Long Bar. Singapore's most famous watering hole is still the favoured place to imbibe a Singapore Sling, created by barman Ngiam Tong Boon (right) early in this century and more recently captured in the painting The Making of a Singapore Sling by French artist Guy Buffet (above left). Another oil painting, Shanghai Lily (top) presides over the bar. It was found in an old Singapore home and was rechristened Shanghai Lily in honour of the original Long Bar in Shanghai.

109

Dining, Singapore style. The cosy interior of Ah Teng's Bakery (above) is lined with rows of antique brass-topped cookie jars, cups and measuring tins. Ah Teng's serves pastries and teas to a steady stream of weary tourists and hungry office workers. The Empire Cafe (right) is a cross between an old-fashioned kopi tiam (a Singapore-style coffee shop) and a modern hotel coffee house. The Singapore-of-yesteryear ambience is created by the marble-topped and tooled teakwood base tables and bentwood-style chairs. The nostalgic mood is heightened by the noisy din as the clatter of bowls and glasses competes with the chatter of diners, the sounds reverberating off marble floors and tiled walls. The eclectic mix of food served reflects Singapore's diverse culinary heritage. Familiar favourites include hearty portions of Chicken Rice, aromatic Nasi Lemak, and a wide variety of fried and soupy noodles, all created to please.